D1309563

STRANGE HISTORIES
THE GREEKS

Fiona Macdonald

◀ *Ancient Greek women dancing, gossiping, playing music, and sitting quietly at home.*

Copyright Permissions
Raintree
100 N. LaSalle St., Ste. 1200
Chicago, IL 60602

Published by Raintree, a division of Reed Elsevier, Inc.

Library of Congress Cataloging-in-Publication Data

Macdonald, Fiona.
  The Greeks / Fiona Macdonald.
    v. cm. -- (Strange histories)
  Includes bibliographical references and index.
  Contents: Meet the Greeks -- Making a living -- The Greeks at home --Family life -- Growing up -- Food and drink -- Looking good -- Fun and games -- Superhuman -- The Greeks at war -- Sickness, death and burial -- Greek facts -- Greek words -- Greek projects.
  ISBN 0-7398-6441-6
  1. Greece--Social life and customs--Juvenile literature. [1. Greece--Social life and customs.] I. Title. II. Series.
DF78.M238 2003
938--dc21
                                        2002155317

Printed in Hong Kong

07 06 05 04 03
10 9 8 7 6 5 4 3 2 1

Acknowledgments
We wish to thank the following individuals and organizations for their help and assistance and for supplying material in their collections: AKG 2 (Peter Connolly), 3 (Peter Connolly), 8 (Peter Connolly), 9 top (Erich Lessing), 11 top (Erich Lessing), 11 bottom (Araldo de Luca), 14 bottom (Erich Lessing), 17 top (Peter Connolly), 18 top (Pirozzi), 20 top (Peter Connolly), 22 (Erich Lessing), 24 both (Erich Lessing), 28 (Erich Lessing), 29 (Erich Lessing); Ancient Art and Architecture Collection 6 both (R Sheridan), 9 bottom (R Sheridan), 14 top (R Sheridan), 21 bottom (R Sheridan); Art Archive 27 bottom (National Archaeological Museum, Athens/Dagli Orti); Bildarchiv Preussicher Kulturbestitz/Antikenmuseum, Berlin) 12 bottom; British Museum, London 10; C M Dixon 1, 4 bottom, 7, 12 top, 13, 17 bottom, 19, 23 top, 25; Corbis 18 bottom (Dave G Houser), 31 (Gianni Dagli Orti); Corbis Digital Stock 5; Digital Vision 26; Mary Evans Picture Library 27 top; Topham Picturepoint 15, 16 top, 21 top, 23 bottom. Artwork by Michael Posen.

LOOK FOR THE STATUE

Look for the statue in boxes like this. Here you will find extra facts, stories, and other interesting information about the strange world of the Greeks.

CONTENTS

▶ *Ancient Greek men fighting, dancing, making sacrifices to the gods, and setting off on a journey.*

MEET THE GREEKS

The Greeks were the most powerful people in Europe from around 600–200 B.C.E.

They were not just powerful but also very proud of their cities, their soldiers, their arts and crafts, their poems and plays, their thinkers, their scientists, and their politicians. They pitied people who were not Greeks and who did not enjoy their civilized Greek way of life.

Greece was divided into many **city-states,** which were cities with farms and countryside around them. All city-states were fierce rivals, and their **citizens** loved to call each other names. Athenians were called "smug and bossy," Spartans were called "cheats and liars," Corinthians were called "soft," and Thebans were called "traitors," which was the worst insult of all.

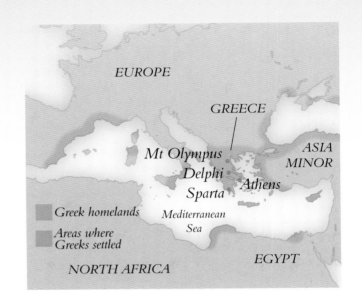

▲ *The ancient Greek homelands. The area shaded in red shows where Greek people lived. Greek families also migrated to settle in colonies all around the Mediterranean Sea in North Africa, Italy, Sicily, and France.*

► *This gold death mask is thought to portray Agamemnon, one of the earliest Greek kings, who ruled the city-state of Mycenae around 1500 B.C.E.*

4

Each city-state had its own laws. Some of these laws were very old. Citizens claimed that they had been made by gods or by mythical kings who probably never existed. (This is not as strange as it sounds; it was a way of saying that the old laws deserved respect.) Other laws were new and led to new types of government. The most important of these was **democracy,** which is a government by the people. It was invented in Athens around 500 B.C.E. However, only male citizens over the age of 30 could take part. Women, foreigners, young men, and **slaves** were banned from participating.

▼ *The Parthenon, the temple of the goddess Athena, stood at the heart of Athens, the most powerful city-state in Greece.*

SPEAK LIKE A GREEK

The ancient Greeks thought their language was the best in the world. They called foreigners "barbarians," because they thought foreign words sounded like sheep bleating, "baa, baa." Following are some ancient Greek words and phrases:

Hello/goodbye: khaire (say "khy-re")
Please: ei soi dokei (say "ay soy dok-ay")
Thank you: kharin oida soi (say "khar-in oy-da soy")
Yes: nai (say "ny")
No: oukhi (say "ook-hi")
Where?: pou (say "poo")
When?: pote (say "po-tay")

Making a Living

Greece was not a comfortable environment. The Greek landscape was wild and mountainous. The Greek climate was harsh, with scorching summers and stormy winters. Worst of all, Greece lay in a violent earthquake zone. Travel over land was very difficult. It was often easier to go by sea, though shipwrecks and pirate attacks were common.

But the Greeks were great survivors. Most people lived in the country and worked on farms. To grow crops, Greek farmers built terraces, which were like steps in steep, rocky hillsides, and dug ditches to carry water from mountain streams.

▲ *This vase shows a Greek boy armed with a stick climbing high into the branches of an olive tree to harvest the ripe fruit (see box, right).*

▼ *The Pleistos Gorge (rocky valley) near Delphi in southern Greece shows the wild, rocky landscape in which the Greeks lived.*

WHY DID GREEK FARMERS HIT THEIR TREES?

Each year, farmers gathered ripe olives by beating the trees until the fruit fell. Then they crushed the olives between stones to get oil. Olive oil was eaten with food, used for cooking, as a skin cleanser and hair conditioner, as a medicine, to soften leather, for burning in lamps, as a prize in sports competitions, and as an offering to the gods.

▼ This terra-cotta (baked clay) statue shows a Greek man sawing wood. Greek farmers usually built their own homes and made their own furniture and farm tools. There were also skilled artisans living in Greek cities who made pottery, jewelry, and fine furniture for citizens to buy.

Farmers' main crops were barley, grapes, and olives. They also grew onions, lettuce, and garlic and kept pigs, sheep, and goats. They went hunting for hares, deer, and even hedgehogs if no other meat could be found. Their wives and children gathered mushrooms, wild fruit, and nuts in the forests, hoping not to meet wild boars or bears.

Farm produce had to last all through the winter. There were no freezers or refrigerators. Cheese was wrapped in leaves or floated in jars of oil. Barley was ground between stones, mixed with oil, seeds, and spices, covered with bran, and stored in wooden tubs. Weeks later, this sticky paste was eaten raw. Even the Greeks did not really like it.

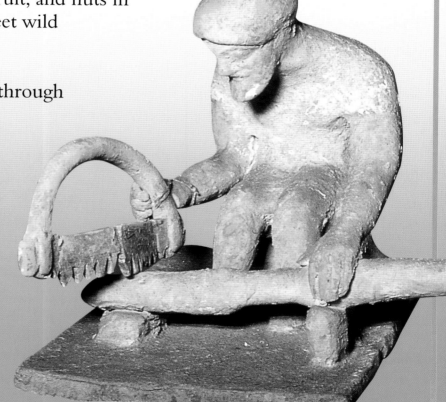

THE GREEKS AT HOME

Greek houses changed size as the families inside them grew. Most ordinary homes began with just a living room and a bedroom, but over the years homeowners added more rooms. All this building work made Greek streets messy and confusing.

Those who could afford to also built new rooms to display their wealth. They added luxuries such as running water from diverted streams. However, because there were no drains, they still used buckets for toilets just like everyone else. They hung woven rugs on the walls and bought carved wooden furniture, including couches, chests, chairs, and low tables.

DANGEROUS AFTER DARK

At night Greek city streets could be dangerous. You might meet prowling robbers, muggers, hooligans, drunken partygoers, or even enemy spies. Or you might trip over people sleeping in doorways, or slip and fall on the rough ground. Wealthy people who needed to go out at night usually took an escort of **slaves** with flaming torches and big sticks.

▶ *This reconstruction drawing is based on the remains of a real Greek house, built in Athens around 450 B.C.E. Only wealthy families could afford a big house like this. Ordinary peoples' homes were much smaller, not as well-built, and often much less tidy.*

Greek families worried about security. There was only one door into a house, and it was guarded by a slave or a dog. Walls (made of mud brick) had to be strong enough to stop "wall-diggers" (burglars) breaking in at night. Privacy was also important. Most houses had a room for women that men could not enter. Men had a separate room of their own for entertaining male friends.

Houses could sometimes seem like prisons. Women, children, and slaves all needed a man's permission to leave. Slaves and women from poor families were allowed out to fetch water or buy food. But women from "respectable" families could only leave to take part in religious ceremonies and funerals or to visit other women. To prevent anyone seeing them, they had to cover their faces with veils.

▼ Hestia (below) was the goddess who guarded Greek homes. The hearth fire in each house was sacred to her. It was very bad luck if it ever went out.

FAMILY LIFE

The Greeks did not have a word for "family." They had "**clans**" and "**households**" instead. A clan meant people descended from one ancestor. A household meant people living together, and might include a married couple, their children, grandparents, servants, and **slaves.**

Greek marriages were often arranged. Brides had no chance to choose a partner or say "no." Husbands and wives may never have met before their wedding day. Once married, they were not equal. Husbands had almost total power over money and legal matters, though wives were in charge of running the home.

NO RIGHTS FOR WOMEN

In ancient Greece, most women could not:
- vote
- serve on juries
- be doctors, lawyers, or teachers
- take part in government
- run big businesses
- own houses and land
- ask for a divorce
- leave their house alone
- talk to men except their close family or slaves

◀ *A mother (left) helps her daughter (right) dress for her wedding. Before leaving her parents' home to live with her new husband, a Greek girl would cut off some or all of her hair and offer it to the goddess Artemis. Then she would veil her face and be carried at night in a torchlight procession to her groom's family home, where she would spend the rest of her married life.*

Parents, grandparents, and children sharing a family meal. Greek households were often large, so poor peoples' small homes were cramped and crowded. To escape, men and boys spent much of their time outside.

The Greeks were fond of children, but babies born to Greek families did not always survive. Their father had the power to decide their fates. He might not want too many boys, since family land would have to be split between them when he died. And girls had to take money to their husband's family when they married. Unwanted babies were abandoned or given to childless couples.

If a father chose to keep a baby, he or she was welcomed with special rituals. Slaves pinned strands of wool (for a girl) or olive twigs (for a boy) to the street door to announce the birth. Then, seven days later, the baby's father picked it up and ran around the hearth with no clothes on! The rest of the household sang hymns. Three days after that, the baby was given a name.

▶ *This Greek statue of a mother and child was made around 300 B.C.E. A wife's main task was to produce a son. If she failed to do this, her husband might divorce her. Greek doctors also thought that having children was good for women's health, even though many Greek women died in childbirth.*

GROWING UP

Only one Greek child in ten learned how to read and write because most did not go to school. Girls stayed at home and learned useful skills such as weaving and cooking from their mothers or from slaves. Boys from poor families had to work and earn money.

If boys did go to school, they were taken there by a **slave.** He stayed with them during lessons and made sure they paid attention. Boys studied reading, writing, math, and lots of poetry. Adults hoped this would teach the children to be brave like the heroes in the poems. They used an **abacus** to do math or worked out the answers in their heads. The Greeks had no signs for numbers, so written sums were impossible.

▲ *Greek parents made their children work hard, but they loved them, too. This tombstone is carved with a touching portrait of a girl who died young, and her pet dog.*

◄ *A Greek schoolboy (center) stands in front of his teacher (left), who is holding a scroll with writing on it. The boy's slave sits on the right. He holds a big stick to punish the boy if he does not learn his lessons well.*

Greek children loved to play, and many of their games and toys were like ours today. They had dolls, rattles, yo-yos, dice, spinning tops, seesaws, and puppets, and they played hockey, tug-of-war, and blind man's bluff. Some of their games were rather different. One favorite was played with sheep anklebones.

Teenagers were kept busy so they would not misbehave. Girls were married at 12 or 14. Teenage boys were made to work or study, or they were sent to sports centers to get healthy exercise. At 18 they had to join the army for two years.

GROWING UP IN SPARTA

In Sparta, a Greek city-state, boys' lives were very hard. At the age of seven, they were taken away from their families to live in army camps. They were kept cold and hungry, and baths were banned. The boys were often beaten. If they died, it proved they were too weak to survive. Spartan girls stayed at home but learned to play tough sports and to fight like boys did.

▼ This bronze statue shows a teenage athlete from Sparta taking part in a race. Her tunic is very short and tight compared with other Greek female clothes (see page 17). The Spartans believed that exercise during youth would help women bear healthy children later in life.

13

FOOD AND DRINK

Greek food was plain and simple. A typical meal might be bread, salted fish, fruit or vegetables, and olive oil. The usual drink, even at breakfast time, was wine mixed with water. Some foreigners said Greek food was boring, but the Greeks despised fancy foods and rich sauces.

Meat was an expensive luxury. Many families looked forward to religious festival days because that was their only chance to eat it. Priests roasted animals that had been **sacrificed** to the gods over fires in front of temples and handed out slices of meat to worshipers. The Greeks also shared another favorite food, barley cakes sweetened with honey, with their gods. Sugar was unknown in ancient Greek times.

▲ *Preparing for a Greek feast. This terra-cotta statue shows a female servant grilling pieces of meat over an open fire.*

◄ *Men relaxing and drinking wine during a symposium (male dinner party). The Greeks always drank wine mixed with water.*

DID ALL GREEK FOOD TASTE GOOD?

The ancient Greeks ate foods that some people might not like today, such as goats' lungs (the air inside whistled as they were cooked), **sea urchins** (raw and still alive) and octopus (very tough and chewy). When food was scarce, in wartime or drought years, Greeks ate almost anything they could find, including iris roots, **beechnuts, lupin** seeds, and grasshoppers.

The Greeks liked cheese but made it from sheep's milk, not cow's. They thought cow's milk was unhealthy. They also enjoyed soups made with lentils and chickpeas. Many Greek people would not eat beans because they believed one **philosopher,** Pythagoras, who claimed that beans contained the souls of the dead.

Normally Greeks ate sitting on low chairs, but on special occasions, such as men-only dinner parties, they ate lying down. Diners relaxed on long, low couches that had room for two, side by side. This was so comfortable that they often dozed off between courses.

▼ *The Greeks used pottery jars to store wine, grain, and oil. When splashed outside with water, they kept the contents cool. Because they were made of clay, mice and rats could not chew their way inside. These massive jars, made on the Greek island of Crete, hold nearly 100 gallons each.*

LOOKING GOOD

Clothes for Greek men, women, and children were all made from a single piece of cloth wrapped round the body and held in place by pins. Underneath, some men wore a **loincloth,** and some women covered their chest with a soft cloth band. But most Greeks wore no underwear at all!

Clothes for men and children were usually knee-length. Women's clothes reached the floor, and so did robes for priests and kings. Most cloth was woven at home from sheep's wool by wives, mothers, and female slaves.

Wealthy people wore fancy cloth woven from Chinese silk and dyed purple with "murex" (rotted shellfish). This cloth could be bought at markets for a high price. Some scholars deliberately wore old, shabby clothes as a sign that they were thinking of more important things. A famous philosopher named Diogenes, who lived around 400–325 B.C.E., gave up clothes altogether and lived in a big pottery jar.

◀ Rich women wore beautiful jewelry made from rare, precious gold, like these earrings made around 250 B.C.E. They might also be buried in special "funeral jewelry," made from thin sheet gold shaped into leaves and flowers, which were signs of rebirth.

Greek women painted their faces with makeup and used hair dye and perfume. They let their hair grow long and tied it back with ribbons or jeweled headbands. Men had short hair and neatly trimmed beards. **Slaves** had their hair cut very short to show they were not free.

▶ *As you can see from these copies of vase paintings, clothes for Greek men, women, and children were all the same basic shape—a loose tube!*

▼ *Greek women and men liked to wear perfume and scented body powder. A few men used makeup and hair dye, too. This perfume flask, made around 500 B.C.E., is shaped like the head of a helmeted soldier.*

MAN-SIZED MEASUREMENTS

The ancient Greeks measured length and distance in units based on an average-sized adult man.

1 finger = 1 in. (2 cm)
4 fingers = 1 palm = 3 in. (7.5 cm)
12 fingers = 1 hand-span = 9 in. (22.5 cm)
16 fingers = 1 foot = 12 in. (30 cm)
24 fingers = 1 cubit = 18 in. (46 cm)
2.5 feet = 1 pace = 30 in. (75 cm)
6 feet = 1 stretch (arms) = 6 ft (1.8 m)
600 feet = 1 stadion = 584 ft (178m)

FUN AND GAMES

The Greeks took life very seriously. They loved to discuss important questions such as, "When did the world begin?" They paid for some of the world's best scientists and smartest thinkers to come and live in their city-states. But they also enjoyed parties, singing, dancing, going to the theater, telling stories, laughing at jokes, and playing games.

Professional storytellers, called "song-stitchers," performed in streets and markets and at festivals. They often added their own extra details to bring the stories up to date. Guests at dinner parties also told jokes and stories and played silly games such as *kottabos,* which involved flicking drops of wine at a target.

◄ *This is a Roman copy of one of the most famous Greek statues ever made. It shows an athlete throwing a discus, a favorite Olympic sport. Sadly, the original has disappeared.*

◄ *This picture shows a Greek amphitheater where plays were performed. The first Greek plays were religious, retelling myths about the gods. Soon they developed into great entertainment that lasted all day long. The audience was mostly men. Greeks believed that tragic plays were too sad for women to watch, and that comic plays were too rude.*

The Greeks liked music and dancing because they were fun. They were also part of many religious ceremonies. Sometimes worshippers got carried away by the music. Stories were told of *maenads,* wild women who left their homes and ran to the mountains, where they tore wild beasts limb from limb.

Sports were the most important form of entertainment. The famous Olympic Games, held in honor of the god Zeus, was just one of many sports festivals open to all Greek athletes. Like football and baseball today, they inspired fierce rivalry and local pride. Champions were sponsored by wealthy businessmen and were rewarded with free food for life by their home city. Winning athletes wore crowns of laurel leaves, pine branches, or wild celery.

FIRST CATCH YOUR TORTOISE

One favorite musical instrument was the lyre. Lyres were used to play solemn, gentle music. They had a U-shaped frame, seven strings, and a sound box that increased the volume. At first their sound boxes were made from tortoise shells, their frames from cattle horns, and their strings from animal gut. Later, lyres were mostly made of wood.

▼ *Chariot racing at the Olympics. A charioteer drives a team of four horses 12 times around a track 3,609 feet (1,100 meters) long. Chariots often crashed and overturned, and drivers died. The winner was the owner of the chariot and horses, not the charioteer who took part in the race.*

SUPERHUMAN

Greek gods and goddesses were like humans, but bigger and better. They were taller, stronger, and more beautiful. They had magic powers and lived forever. Many gods helped their favorite people or cities, but they could also be mischievous, fierce, and cruel.

To keep the gods happy, the Greeks offered them presents, called **sacrifices.** At first these were real people. Young girls were the usual sacrifice when an army set off for war. Later, the Greeks offered animals, food, or wine.

The Greeks built huge temples but they didn't go inside. A temple was a god's house and was too holy for anyone other than priests and priestesses to enter. A few gods and goddesses were worshiped secretly, in the countryside or in hidden caves. Some special underground rituals to honor Demeter, goddess of fertility, were so mysterious that no one knows what went on, even today. Anyone who tried to tell was killed instantly.

▶ *This is a modern reconstruction of the statue of the mighty goddess Athena that stood in the Parthenon temple in Athens (see page 5). The original was made of gold and ivory and was about 33 feet (10 meters) high.*

A-Z OF GODS AND GODDESSES

This "family" of gods and goddesses lived on Olympus, the highest mountain in Greece.

Aphrodite – goddess of love and beauty
Apollo – god of music and learning
Ares – god of war
Artemis – goddess of young girls and wild creatures
Athena – goddess of wisdom, art and craft, and war
Demeter – goddess of grain and growing crops
Dionysus – god of wine and wildness
Hera – goddess of women and marriage
Hermes – messenger of the gods
Hestia – goddess of hearths and homes
Poseidon – god of earthquakes and the sea
Zeus – god of lightning, king of the gods

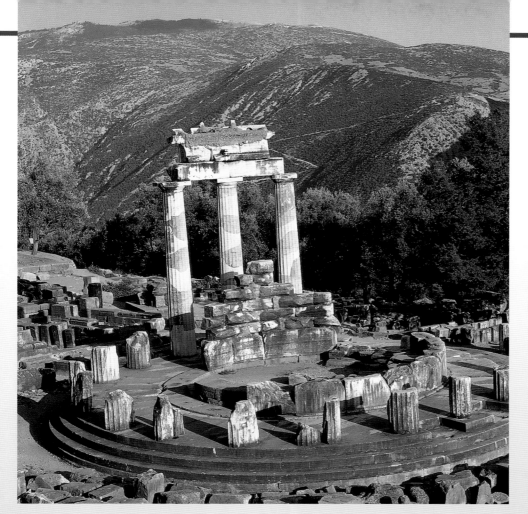

◄ A ruined temple at Delphi, one of the holiest places in Greece. Temples were shaped like the first Greek houses. Their stone columns were copies of the tree trunks that held up the house roofs.

▼ Worshipers taking part in mysterious ceremonies to honor the goddess Demeter. They believed that she had the power to make them happy in the life after death.

Spirits living in fields, streams, and trees were also worshiped by the Greeks. They believed that some spirits, called **oracles,** could see into the future. Priests talked to oracle trees and hung prayers in their branches. They also examined the guts of dead animals for omens. At Delphi a priestess, drugged with smoke from burning leaves, gave answers to questions. People believed the oracle spoke through her words.

THE GREEKS AT WAR

The Greeks were fierce warriors but they usually fought themselves. Rival **city-states** quarreled over land and trade. Great cities were destroyed and many brave people died. Twice the Greeks united, more or less, to defeat their great enemies, the Persians. They also fought against the Turkish city of Troy.

Most wars were short. Fighting stopped in late summer because soldiers had to help with harvesting, and again in winter because the weather was too cold. Only the warlike city of Sparta stayed ready to fight year-round. Unlike other Greeks, Spartan soldiers wore uniforms and marched to music. The noise of Spartan flute-players could be deafening. Mothers in Sparta wanted their sons to be brave. Before a battle they told them, "come back carrying your shield [that is, fit and victorious] or on it [dead!]."

◄ *Famous hero Alexander the Great (see page 27) fighting against the Persians at the Battle of Issus in 333 B.C.E. Against the odds, he led Greek and Macedonian soldiers to victory against the much larger Persian army.*

◀ *Greek soldiers' metal armor was tough and strong, but it was also very heavy. Each man's gear could weigh over 66 pounds (30 kilograms).*

THE BEST WAY TO WIN?

The Greeks invented fearsome war machines, such as giant crossbows armed with iron-tipped arrows and huge catapults that hurled lumps of rock at enemy walls. They even made **flamethrowers.** Still, many Greek soldiers preferred traditional tactics in war. They destroyed crops and cut down olive trees to starve the enemy. They surrounded cities until food and water ran out or until the citizens all died of disease.

All **citizens** were meant to serve as soldiers, but poor men could not afford to. Each Greek **hoplite** (infantryman) had to buy his own shield, helmet, breastplate, spear, sword, and **greaves** (shinguards). If poor men did go to war, they fought with cheap weapons like slingshots and had no protection from enemy attack.

▼ *Powerful Greek city-states built heavy warships, similar to the modern reconstruction in the picture, to fight against enemy fleets. They were powered by sailes and by men rowing. Each ship was armed with a metal-tipped battering ram at the prow (front), designed to smash holes in enemy ships and sink them.*

SICKNESS, DEATH, AND BURIAL

The Greeks used magic, medicine, religious ceremonies, and sometimes science to try to cure disease. Most of them still died young. The average Greek woman lived until she was 35 years old. A man might live longer, maybe to the age of 50. Many children died before they were 5 years old.

Greek doctors thought that people had four different liquids, or humors, flowing through their bodies— red blood, green phlegm, yellow bile, and black choler—and that too much of any one caused disease. They tested and even tasted samples to diagnose illnesses.

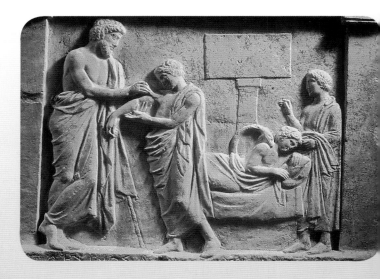

▲ *Many Greek people believed that sickness was sent by the gods. They slept overnight at healing shrines (above) hoping that Asclepius, the god of healing, or his magic snake would visit them in a dream and cure them.*

One famous doctor had different ideas. His name was Hippocrates (about 460–370 B.C.E.). He studied his patients scientifically and said that illness was caused by an unhealthy lifestyle or an unquiet mind. He also said doctors should be clean, neat, slim, sweet smelling, and good-looking! Patients would trust them more that way.

If doctors failed to cure a patient, the body of the deceased had to be buried. Greek funerals took place at dawn and were very noisy occasions. Women wept and wailed, scratched their cheeks and cut their hair. After the body was buried, offerings of food were placed on its tomb for nine days. Then the dishes were broken to stop the ghost from coming back for more!

▲ *Many Greek tombstones were decorated with scenes from the dead person's life. Here, a woman called Hegeso, who died in the 4th century B.C.E., is shown with her female **slave** (left), who is handing her a box of jewelry.*

◄ *The Greek women on this piece of pottery are preparing a corpse for burial while mourners on either side pray, weep, and wail. The Greeks usually raised their hands in the air when praying to the gods, because most of the gods lived high above in the sky.*

THREE STAGES OF LIFE

Greek legends describe a terrifying monster called the Sphinx. It lay in wait for travellers and would not let them pass until they had answered this riddle: "What has four legs, then two, then three?" The answer was "a human" because a baby crawls on four legs, an adult walks on two legs, and an old person walks with a stick. If anyone answered wrong, the Sphinx ate them.

GREEK FACTS

Here is a selection of interesting facts about the strange world of the ancient Greeks.

MEN ONLY

Women were banned at the Olympic Games, but one mother was so keen to see her son race that she dressed as a man and hid among the crowd. When she saw her son winning, she shouted out with excitement and gave herself away. She was expelled in disgrace.

TRICKSTER

Athenian ruler Peisistratus (about 600–527 B.C.E.) seized power by a clever trick. He rushed into town one day, covered in mud and bruises, claiming to have been attacked. He asked the citizens' assembly to give him a bodyguard, and they agreed. He used this bodyguard to defeat his enemies and take control of the city.

SMELLY FEET

Priests at the temple of Zeus at Dodona, southern Greece, were known as *selloi*, which means "with unwashed feet." No one knows why they were so dirty!

▲ *Greek ideas, discoveries, and artistic styles still shape our lives today. Many special buildings, like the White House (above), the home of the president, are designed to look like ancient Greek structures.*

MARATHON MAN

In ancient Greece fast runners carried urgent wartime messages. The most famous was Pheidippides. It was said that he ran 26 miles (42 kilometers) from a battlefield at Marathon in 490 B.C.E. to tell the Athenians that their army had defeated the Persians. He then died from exhaustion!

LUCKY FOR SOME

For the Greeks, right was lucky and left was unlucky. When Greek general Xenophon (about 435–354 B.C.E.) was preparing for battle in 401 B.C.E., he heard an eagle screeching on his right-hand side. Priests told him this meant he would win. He did.

THE WORLD'S GREATEST WARRIOR?

Most Greeks thought Alexander the Great (356–323 B.C.E.) was the greatest soldier who ever lived. Some said he was a god. Alexander became king of Macedonia (north of Greece) when he was only 20 years old. Then he set off to conquer the world. He won a vast empire, stretching from Greece and Egypt to India and Afghanistan. He wanted more, but his army refused to march any farther. He died in Iraq at age 32.

THE ANCIENT GREEKS VISITED GREAT BRITAIN

Explorer Pytheas reached Orkney and Shetland in Britain around 350 B.C.E. The Greeks also sailed along the coast of Africa and may have crossed the Equator.

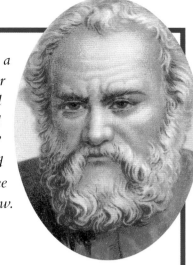

▶ *Archimedes invented a machine to make water flow uphill. It is still used today, and is called the "Archimedian screw" because it turns around and around like a corkscrew.*

I'VE GOT IT!

Greek mathematician and inventor Archimedes (287–212 B.C.E.) was one of the greatest scientists of all time. After he discovered how pulleys and levers work, he boasted, "Give me somewhere to stand, and I will move the Earth!" He also became famous for making a very important discovery about mass and gravity while he was in his bath. He was so excited that he jumped out and ran down the street shouting "Eureka!" (I've got it!).

◀ *Greek athletes wrestling. The most violent Greek sport was* pankration *("total power"), which was a mixture of boxing and wrestling with no holds barred except biting and eye-gouging!*

GREEK WORDS

This glossary explains some of the words used in this book that you might not have seen before.

abacus wooden frame with rows of beads, used as an early kind of calculator

assembly meeting of citizens in a city-state

beechnuts small, brown, bitter, chewy nuts from beech trees

citizen person living in a city-state who had full rights to take part in government and help make laws

city-state city and the surrounding land that it controlled

clan people descended from one ancestor. They had a duty to help one another.

democracy government by the people

flamethrower long tube that shoots jets of flame

greaves shinguards. They were like football shin-pads but made of metal.

▲ *A hoplite (foot-soldier) in a hurry! Many Greek soldiers decorated their shields with symbols of their city-state. This made it easier to recognize friends or enemies in battle.*

hoplites soldiers in heavy armor who fought on foot

household people living in the same home

loincloth strip of cloth wound around the lower body

lupin flowering plant. The seeds are poisonous, so do not eat them.

mythical from a story explaining a custom or natural phenomenon; not necessarily true

omen sign of what is to come in the future

oracle spirit that can see into the future and give advice

philosopher a highly educated person. Philosophers were often in charge of respected places of learning.

sacrifice offering to the gods, to give thanks or to ask for help

sea urchin soft, pulpy creature that lives on the ocean floor. Urchins are covered by a dome-shaped shell.

slave man, woman, or children who were not free but belonged to their owners. They could be bought and sold. Some were treated well, others were treated badly.

▼ *Many Greek myths tell fantastic and funny stories about gods and heroes. Here, the hero Heracles is hiding in a big storage jar from a three-headed monster dog called Cerberus, who guarded the way into the Underworld.*

Greek Projects

If you want to find out more about the Greeks, here are some ideas for projects.

Make a water clock

The ancient Greeks did not have clocks with springs, batteries or electricity. They used water clocks, called *clepsydra*, instead. Here is how to make one. It might be best to try this outside since it could be messy.

You will need:
two plastic containers, both about the same size (You could use big yogurt cartons or the bottom halves of two soft drink bottles.)
a bendy drinking straw, scissors, plastic bricks or a plastic box, a small piece of plastic food wrap, a small rubber band, water

1. Using scissors, carefully make a small hole in one of the containers, near the bottom. It should be just big enough for the straw to fit in.
2. Trim the straw so it looks like the straw in the diagram.
3. Push one end of the straw into the hole. Cover the other end with food wrap. Use the rubber band to hold the wrap in place.

4. Stand the container on the bricks or box. Put the other container below it, as shown.
5. Fill the top container with water and carefully remove the food wrap and elastic band.
6. See how long the water takes to run out into the lower container. It will be the same every time.

PAINT BACK-TO-FRONT, GREEK-STYLE

Greek artisans liked to decorate the pots they made with scenes from everyday life or with pictures of gods and heroes. They often used a special back-to-front technique:

1. They drew the outline of the gods or people they wanted to show.
2. They painted the background black, leaving the rest unpainted.
3. Sometimes they added details, like eyes or hair, to the unpainted area.

You will need:

colored paper, a pen or pencil, black paint, a brush

Follow steps 1 to 3 above and see if you can paint back-to-front in the Greek way.

ENJOY SOME ANCIENT GREEK STORIES

Many stories told by Greek "song-stitchers" are still popular today. You can find them in your school or public library. Look out for books telling the strange adventures of Greek hero Odysseus and all the magical monsters he met. Or read about brave Greek soldiers and how they conquered their enemies at Troy by using a very clever trick.

▲ *This picture from a Greek pot shows the god Zeus marrying the goddess Hera. The spirit of Love (with wings) is placing a crown of flowers on Zeus's head.*

GREEKS ON THE INTERNET

The Internet is a great way to find out more about the Greeks. However, the Internet is constantly changing, so if you can't find these websites try searching using the word "Greeks."

http://www.historyforkids.org/learn/greeks/index.htm

http://www.museum.upenn.edu/Greek_World/Index.html

http://www.upenn.edu/museum/Olympics/olympicintro.html

http://www.perseus.tufts.edu/Olympics

http://www.aesopfables.com/

INDEX